AF593821

121 High Street, Berkhamsted, Herts

First edition 1974
Reprinted 1975
Reprinted 1976
Reprinted 1977

ISBN 0 85648 021 5

Photographs by David Alexander

Quotations from Good News Bible: Today's English Version, *copyright 1971 American Bible Society; by permission of the Bible Societies*

Printed in Great Britain by Sackville Press, Billericay, Essex

A song of glory

THE WINGS OF THE WIND

Praise the Lord, my soul!
Lord, my God, how great you are!
You are clothed with majesty and glory;
you cover yourself with light.
You stretched out the heavens like a tent,
and built your home on the waters above.
You use the clouds as your chariot,
and walk on the wings of the wind.
You use the winds as your messengers.
and flashes of lightning as your servants . . .

May the glory of the Lord last for ever!
May the Lord be happy with what he made!
He looks at the earth, and it trembles;
he touches the mountains, and they pour
out smoke.

I will sing to the Lord all my life;
I will sing praises to my God as long as I live.

From PSALM 104

Mountains, trees, sky and setting sun combine to express the glory of God's creation.

ETERNAL GOD AND MORTAL MAN

Lord, you have always been our home.
Before the hills were created,
before you brought the world into being,
you are eternally God, without beginning or end.

Our lifetime is cut short by your anger;
our life comes to an end like a whisper.
Seventy years is all we have –
eighty years, if we are strong;
yet all they bring us is worry and trouble;
life is soon over, and we are gone.

Who really knows the full power of your anger?
Who knows what fear your fury can bring?
Teach us how short our life is,
so that we may become wise . . .

From PSALM 90

The rock mountains of the desert of Judea form the background for the vivid colour of trees in the oasis of Ein Gedi.

THE VOICE OF GOD

The Lord's voice is heard on the seas;
the glorious God thunders,
and his voice echoes over the ocean.
The Lord's voice is heard
in all its might and majesty!

The Lord's voice breaks the cedars,
even the cedars of Lebanon.
He causes the mountains of Lebanon to jump like calves,
and Mount Hermon to leap like a young bull.

The Lord's voice makes the lightning flash.
His voice makes the desert shake;
he shakes the desert of Kadesh.
The Lord's voice makes the deer give birth,
and leaves the trees stripped bare,
while in his temple all shout, 'Glory to God!'

From PSALM 29

Mediterranean breakers by the ruins of Caesarea.

NO OTHER GOD

Listen, Lord, to my prayer;
hear my cries for help.
I call to you in times of trouble,
because you answer my prayer.

There is no other god like you, Lord,
not one who can do what you can do.
All the nations you have created
will come and bow down to you.
They will praise your greatness,
because only you, God, are mighty;
only you do wonderful things.

From PSALM 86

The simple, brilliant colour of poppies against the waters of a mountain stream.

THE WONDER OF GOD'S LOVE

Lord, your constant love reaches the heavens,
your faithfulness extends to the skies.
Your righteousness is firm like the great mountains,
your judgements are like the depths of the sea.
You, Lord, care for men and animals.

How precious, God, is your constant love!
Men find protection under the shadow of your wings.
They feast on the abundant food from your house;
you give them to drink from the river of your goodness.
You are the source of all life,
and because of your light we see the light.

From PSALM 36

Two buzzards soar above Mount Gilboa; in the distance beyond the hills of Galilee the long range of Mount Hermon.

FLING WIDE THE GATES

The world and all that is in it belong
to the Lord;
the earth and all who live on it are his.
He built it on the deep waters beneath the earth
and laid its foundations in the ocean depths.

Who has the right to go up the Lord's hill?
Who is allowed to enter his holy temple?
He who is pure in act and in thought,
who does not worship idols,
or make false promises.
The Lord will bless him;
God his Saviour will declare him innocent.
Such are the people who come to God,
who come into the presence of the God of Jacob

Fling wide the gates,
open the ancient doors,
and the great king will come in!
Who is this great king?
He is the Lord, strong and mighty,
the Lord, victorious in battle!

Fling wide the gates,
open the ancient doors,
and the great king will come in!
Who is this great king?
The Lord of armies, he is the great king!

PSALM 24

A 'shofar' or ram's horn, of the type used in ancient
Israel to call to battle or proclaim the king (from
the Haifa Music Museum).

THE LORD IS KING!

The Lord is king!
He is clothed with majesty,
and covered with strength.
Surely the earth is set firmly in place
and cannot be moved.
Your throne, Lord, has been firm from the beginning,
and you existed before time began.

The ocean depths raise their voice, Lord;
they raise their voice and roar.
The Lord rules supreme in heaven,
greater than the roar of the ocean,
more powerful than the waves of the sea.

Your laws are eternal, Lord,
and your temple is holy indeed,
for ever and ever.

PSALM 93

The sun setting above the Aegean coast of southern Greece.

TO GOD BE THE GLORY

To you alone, Lord, to you alone,
and not to us, must glory be given,
because of your constant love and
faithfulness.

Why should the nations ask us,
'Where is your God?'
Our God is in heaven,
doing whatever he wishes.
Their gods are made of silver and gold,
formed by human hands . . .

Trust in the Lord, people of Israel!
He helps you and protects you.
Trust in the Lord, you priests of God!
He helps you and protects you.
Trust in the Lord, all who fear him!
He helps you and protects you.

From PSALM 115

A group of women at a well in the hills of Judea.

I WILL TELL OF GOD'S GREATNESS

I will proclaim your greatness, my God and king;
I will thank you for ever and ever.
Every day I will thank you;
I will praise you for ever and ever.
The Lord is great, and must be highly praised;
his greatness is beyond understanding.

What you have done will be praised from one generation to the next;
they will proclaim your mighty acts.
Men will speak of your glory and majesty,
and I will meditate on your wonderful deeds.

Men will speak of your mighty acts,
and I will proclaim your greatness.
They will tell about all your goodness,
and sing about your kindness.

From PSALM 145

A donkey-rider returns home from a day in the fields, as the sun sets behind the hills of Galilee.

ALL PEOPLES SEE GOD'S GLORY

The Lord is king! Be glad, earth!
Rejoice, all you islands of the seas!
Clouds and darkness are round him;
his kingdom is based on righteousness and justice.
Fire goes in front of him,
and burns up his enemies around him.
His lightning lights up the world;
the earth sees it and trembles.
The hills melt like wax before the Lord,
before the Lord of all the earth.
The heavens proclaim his righteousness,
and all peoples see his glory.

From PSALM 97

The sun bathes the ruins of the ancient city of Avdat with glory.

TREMBLE, EARTH

When the people of Israel left Egypt,
when Jacob's descendants left that foreign land,
Judah became the Lord's holy people,
Israel became his own possession.

The Sea of Reeds looked and ran away,
the Jordan River stopped flowing.
The mountains skipped like goats,
the hills skipped around like sheep.

What happened, Sea, to make you run away?
And you, Jordan, why did you stop flowing?
Mountains, why did you skip like goats?
Hills, why did you skip around like sheep?

Tremble, earth, at the Lord's coming,
at the presence of the God of Jacob,
who changes rocks into pools of water,
and stone cliffs into flowing springs.

PSALM 114

A desert nomad looking across to the mountains of Sinai, scene of Israel's wandering in the wilderness and giving of the law.

GOD'S WONDERS

I will remember your great acts, Lord;
I will recall the wonders you did in the past.
I will think about all that you have done;
I will meditate on all your deeds.

Everything you do, God, is holy!
No god is as great as you!
You are the God who works miracles;
you showed your might among the nations.
By your power you saved your people,
the descendants of Jacob and of Joseph.

When the waters saw you, God, they were
afraid,
and the depths of the sea trembled .
The clouds poured down rain;
thunder crashed from the sky,
and lightning flashed in all directions.
The crash of your thunder rolled out,
and flashes of lightning lit up the whole world;
the earth trembled and shook.

You walked through the sea;
you crossed the deep ocean,
but your footprints could not be seen.
You led your people like a shepherd,
with Moses and Aaron in charge of them.

From PSALM 77

The sun behind an acacia bush, one of the few trees to survive in the heat of the Sinai desert.

THE GLORY OF GOD'S WORLD

You make springs flow in the valleys,
and water run between the hills.
They provide water for the wild animals;
the wild donkeys quench their thirst;
in the trees near by
the birds make their nests and sing.

From heaven you send rain on the mountains,
and the earth is filled with your blessings.
You make grass grow for the cattle,
and plants for man to use,
so he can grow his crops,
and produce wine to make him happy,
olive oil to make him cheerful,
and bread to give him strength.

You created the moon to mark the months;
the sun knows the time to set.
You made the night, and in the darkness
all the wild animals come out . . .

Lord, you have made so many things!
How wisely you have made them all! . . .

Praise the Lord, my soul!
Praise the Lord!

From PSALM 104

A stream flowing from the mountains of Galilee.

THE GLORY OF MAN

Lord, our Lord,
your greatness is seen in all the world!
Your praise reaches up to the heavens;
it is sung by children and babies.
You have built a fortress against your foes
to stop your enemies and adversaries.

When I look at the sky, which you have made,
at the moon and the stars, which you set in
their places –
what is man, that you think of him;
mere man, that you care for him?
Yet you made him inferior only to yourself;
you crowned him with glory and honour.
You made him ruler over all you have made;
you placed him over all things:
sheep and cattle, and wild animals too;
the birds and the fish,
and all the creatures in the seas.

Lord, our Lord,
your greatness is seen in all the world!

PSALM 8

A rider in the vastness of the Syrian desert, alone beneath the sky.

GOD'S GLORY IN CREATION

How clearly the sky reveals God's glory!
How plainly it shows what he has done!
Each day announces it to the following day;
each night repeats it to the next.
No speech or words are used,
no sound is heard;
yet their voice goes out to all the world,
their message reaches the ends of the earth.

God set up a tent in the sky for the sun;
it comes out like a bridegroom striding
from his house,
like an athlete, eager to run a race.
It starts at one end of the sky
and goes round to the other.
Nothing can hide from its heat.

From PSALM 19

The sun rises over the Gulf of Eilat.

GOD'S GLORIOUS LAW

The law of the Lord is perfect;
it gives new life.
The commands of the Lord are trustworthy,
giving wisdom to those who lack it.
The rules of the Lord are right,
and those who obey them are happy.
His commandments are completely just
and give understanding to the mind.
The worship of the Lord is good;
it will continue for ever.
The judgements of the Lord are just,
they are always fair.
They are more desirable than gold,
even the finest gold.
They are sweeter than honey,
even the purest honey.
They give knowledge to me, your servant;
I am rewarded for obeying them.

From PSALM 19

God's law was for ordinary people for all time: an orange-seller beneath a Roman arch at Tarsus.

WHEN THE WORLD WAS MADE

The Lord created the heavens by his command,
the sun, moon, and stars by his spoken word.
He gathered all the seas into one place;
he shut up the ocean depths in store-rooms.

Fear the Lord, all the earth!
Fear him, all peoples of the world!
When he spoke, the world was created;
at his command everything appeared.

From PSALM 33

The Mediterranean coast of southern Turkey.

GOD REIGNS

The Lord is king;
the people tremble;
he sits on his throne on the cherubim;
the earth shakes.
The Lord is mighty in Zion;
he rules over all the nations.
Everyone will praise his great and majestic
name.
Holy is he!

Mighty king, you love what is right;
you have brought justice to Israel;
you have brought righteousness and fairness.
Praise the Lord our God;
worship before his throne!
Holy is he!

From PSALM 99

A gateway into the old city of Jerusalem, ancient Zion.

THE RIGHTEOUS JUDGE

The Almighty God, the Lord, speaks;
he calls to the whole earth, from east to west.
God shines from Zion,
the city perfect in its beauty.

Our God is coming, but not in silence;
a raging fire is in front of him,
a furious storm round him.
He calls heaven and earth as witnesses
to see him judge his people.
He says, 'Gather my faithful people to me,
those who made a covenant with me by
offering a sacrifice.'
The heavens proclaim that God is righteous,
that he himself is judge!

From PSALM 50

Towers of Zion, city of David.

GOD IS THE SAME FOR EVER

My life is like the evening shadows;
I am like dry grass.

But you, Lord, are king for ever;
all generations will remember you . . .

Lord, you live for ever;
long ago you created the earth,
and with your own hands you made the heavens.
They will all disappear, but you will remain;
they will all wear out like clothes.
You will change them like clothes, and they will vanish;
but you are always the same, and your life never ends.
Our children will live in safety,
and their descendants will always live
under your protection.

From PSALM 102

Behind the parched, dry grass – the sun.